A souvenir guide

Claremont Landscape Garden

Surrey

Welcome	
The Duke	
Robert Clive of India	14
Royal Claremont	16
The National Trust	24

National Trust

Welcome to Claremont

In the eighteenth century, Claremont was among the most famous landscape gardens in Europe.

In 1714 Thomas Pelham-Holles bought the Claremont estate from architect, playwright and spy Sir John Vanbrugh. The house and garden increased in size and splendour during the following 50 years, reflecting the grandeur of its owner, who became the Duke of Newcastle-upon-Tyne in 1715.

Owned briefly by Robert Clive of India, who built the house here today (not National Trust), Claremont was a royal residence from

Who owned and lived at Claremont?

1709–14	Sir John Vanbrugh
1714–69	Thomas, 1st Duke of Newcastle and his widow Harriot
1769–86	Robert, Lord Clive and his widow, Margaret, Lady Clive
1786–7	Robert, 4th Viscount Galway
1787–1802	2nd Earl and Countess of Tyrconnel
1802–16	Charles Rose Ellis
1816–65	Charlotte, Princess of Wales (d.1817) and her widower, Leopold, Prince of Saxe-Coburg-Saalfeld
1865–1901	Queen Victoria
1848–66	Louis-Philippe, former King of the French, and his family
1879–1922	Prince Leopold, Duke of Albany, and his widow, Helen
1922–6	Sir William Corry, 2nd Bt
1925–6	Co-Owners Ltd
1926–30	Claremont Estates
1930	Eugene Speyer
1930–31	Percy Rampton and William Hoptroff
1931–49	Sir Samuel Hanson Ramsbotham (garden only)
1947–	The National Trust (garden only)

Left Thomas, Duke of Newcastle, who made Claremont one of the great gardens of mid-eighteenth-century Europe; pastel portrait by William Hoare, c.1752 (National Portrait Gallery). The Duke christened the estate 'Claremont' after one of his subsidiary titles – Earl of Clare

1816 until 1922, after which the estate was broken up for development.

At its largest, 1,500 acres once surrounded the house at Claremont, made up of the pleasure ground, flower garden, ponds, woods, a farm and deer-park, and a vast kitchen garden which produced fruit and vegetables for the family.

Welcome to Claremont

Left The Amphitheatre – a series of semi-circular turf terraces – was created by the garden designer Charles Bridgeman about 1722

Above The Grotto, the Belisle garden pavilion and exotic birds from the Duke of Newcastle's Claremont menagerie appear in this tapestry panel, which was woven in Fulham about 1754 (Clandon Park)

'How well Claremont agreed with me that my Friends must come down to see me here, and I hope to believe they will.'
  Duke of Newcastle writing to his wife, 1766

The Duke of Newcastle

Thomas, Duke of Newcastle (1693–1768) was rich beyond most people's wildest dreams and held immense political power. But both money and influence had a habit of disappearing through his fingers.

'All sorts of fruit in perfection.'
The Duke of Newcastle

The Duke of N~~ewcast~~le and his Cook.

Above The Duke of Newcastle lamenting the loss of his French chef, Pierre de St Clouet, who demanded the huge salary of 100 guineas a year. This cartoon of 1745 satirised the Duke's well-known fondness for fancy French food

Left Adam Taylor's *A treatise on the ananas or pine-apple* (1769). The Duke had a passion for pineapples

Mad for gardening, fanatical about fruit

In 1714 the Duke, aged just 21, bought Claremont from its owner and architect Sir John Vanbrugh. He retained Vanbrugh as his architect, trebling the size of the house and adding a 74-foot-long Great Room in which he held grand dinners and entertained foreign ambassadors. The Duke also landscaped and planted the gardens, which became famous across Europe. The kitchen garden was a massive six acres, producing the 'most delicious fruits of every kind'.

Away from the stresses of London, the Duke and his wife Harriot would picnic on the island, sometimes eating too much ripe fruit, which had unwelcome results. The status and joy of growing pineapples were so important to the Duke that, even when faced with financial ruin, he wrote, 'I can never think of parting with my pineapples'.

Vanbrugh has to resort to fruity language to get the new roof finished at Claremont

'As to the Building at Claremont: I am Swearing as much as is necessary to get it cover'd.'

Vanbrugh to the Duke of Newcastle, 27 November 1716

The Duke of Newcastle and his designers
The evolution of a garden

The Duke of Newcastle loved Claremont and used the garden and house to impress his family and friends, his political cronies and enemies.

Keeping up with the latest fashion in garden design was very important to the Duke. He employed a succession of the best designers of their day: Sir John Vanbrugh, Charles Bridgeman and finally William Kent. Vanbrugh added many garden buildings to the landscape, but the only one that survives is the Belvedere. Bridgeman created the Amphitheatre. Kent may have been responsible for designing the original Thatched Cottage and Belisle, the island in the lake with the garden pavilion that stands on it. Successive members of the Greening family and a large staff looked after the garden.

In 1720 the pond would have been circular with formal trees planted on its edge and an obelisk at its centre. By 1738 this had been transformed into the informal lake you see today, with an arched cascade at one end. In 1750 Newcastle made this into a grotto and towards the end of his life had the Amphitheatre 'planted as thick as possible with Shrubs'.

'Just going to Belisle. My dearest will admire this charming place more than you imagine.'

The Duke of Newcastle

Above Belisle. The island pavilion was probably designed by William Kent and was finished by 1740. The Duke used it for writing letters and *al fresco* dining (it had its own kitchen)

Left The lake

Right The architect Sir John Vanbrugh designed the Belvedere and sold Claremont to the Duke of Newcastle in 1714; painted by Sir Godfrey Kneller about 1704–10 (National Portrait Gallery)

Below The Grotto was built in 1750

> 'That seems the happy Work of Nature; such is its elegant Rusticity.'
> Henrietta Pye on the Grotto, 1760

The Duke of Newcastle

8 A place of escape from the corridors of power

'I begg you would order hott Rolls for bread & butter, Ice Cream, & some cold Ham & Chickens, you will therefore order a Ham to be boiled tomorrow for Cold, & some chickens to be roasted, we will have fruit & these things on the Island, lett Prevost make some Cherry water & some Leomanade in Ice.'

Duke of Newcastle to his wife

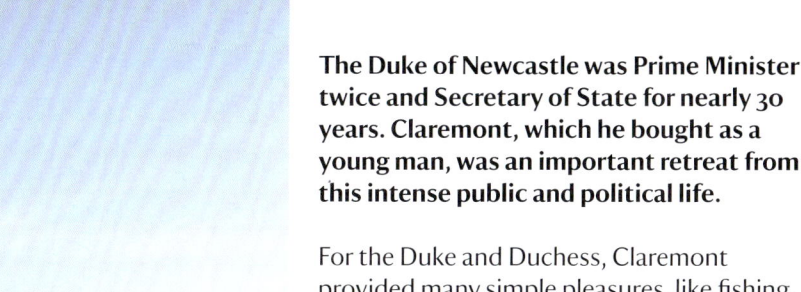

The Duke of Newcastle was Prime Minister twice and Secretary of State for nearly 30 years. Claremont, which he bought as a young man, was an important retreat from this intense public and political life.

For the Duke and Duchess, Claremont provided many simple pleasures, like fishing, boating on the lake or enjoying the view from the top of the Amphitheatre.

This is where the Duke and Duchess, their friends and family came to play bowls and to admire the Belvedere, a focal point in the garden. The tower was a place to write letters, have supper parties and play cards. A telescope on the roof allowed star gazing and inspecting the houses and estates of their neighbours. The Duke seems to have used the Thatched Cottage for gambling. (The present building is a late nineteenth-century replacement.)

Above The Thatched Cottage

Left The Belvedere was a meeting place for the Kit-Cat Club, a dining club to which both the Duke and Vanbrugh belonged

Far left The view from the top of the Amphitheatre

A walk in the park

On the advice of his doctor, the Duke of Newcastle, by this time in his mid-70s, took a walk each day when he was at Claremont, and afterwards wrote to his wife Harriot about what he had seen.

The Duke's regular walks took him up the steep path that runs along the north side of the Amphitheatre and which he christened 'Bridgeman's Walk', after garden designer Charles Bridgeman, who made the

Below John Rocque's survey plan of the garden was made in 1743, but not published until 1750

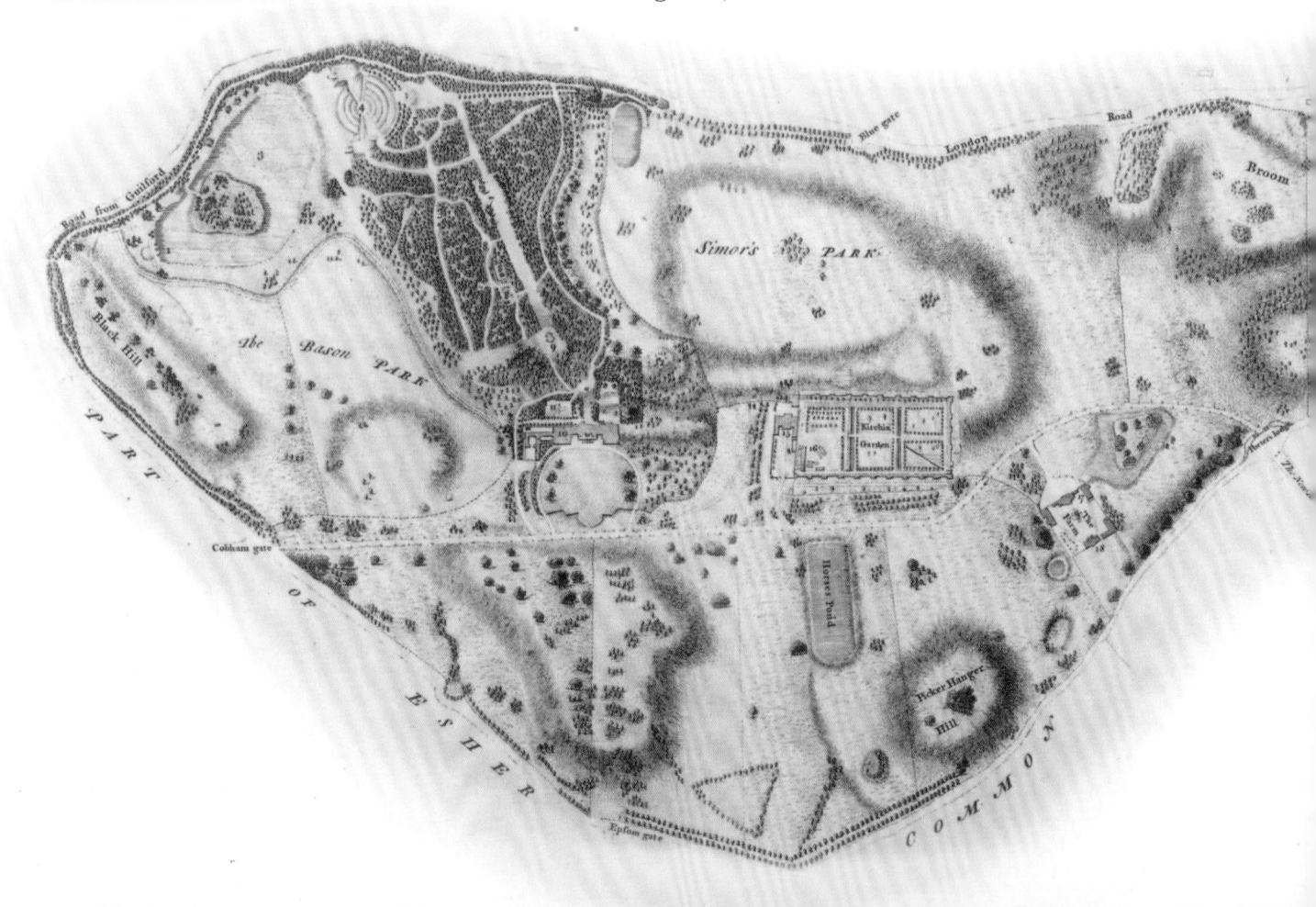

Right The Ha-ha separated the pleasure ground from Bason Park. It took its present form in the 1770s

Below right The Duchess of Newcastle; by Jonathan Richardson (private collection). The Duke and Duchess enjoyed a very happy marriage

Overleaf The Amphitheatre from across the lake

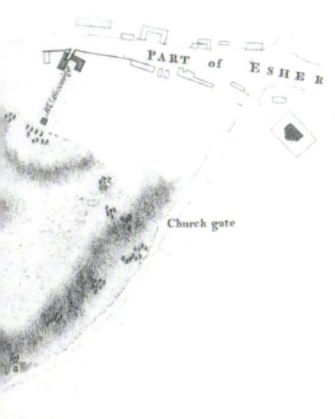

Amphitheatre and laid out the pleasure ground in the 1720s. The National Trust does not own the remaining length of the path, which would have led you back to the Duke's house.

The Duke and Duchess of Newcastle created Claremont for their pleasure and that of their friends. They were childless, and the development and care of the garden became rather like a substitute family.

'Dear Claremont was never in greater beauty. Every thing green, the trees charmingly come out, the wood delightful. The cuckoo and nightingale have made their appearance and Mr. Hurdis has seen *two swallows*. I wanted nothing but my dearest here.'

The Duke of Newcastle to his wife, 28 April 1765

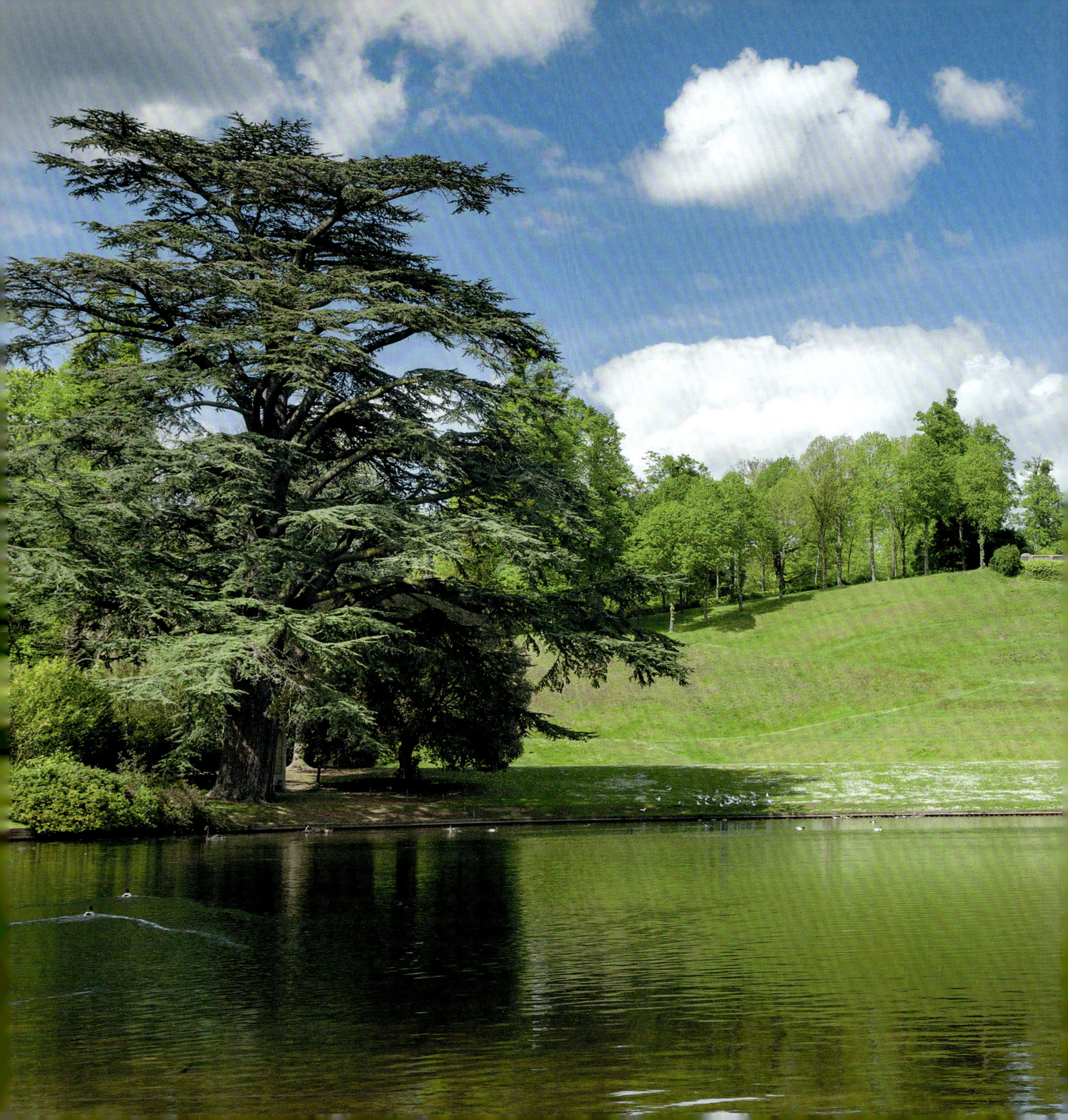

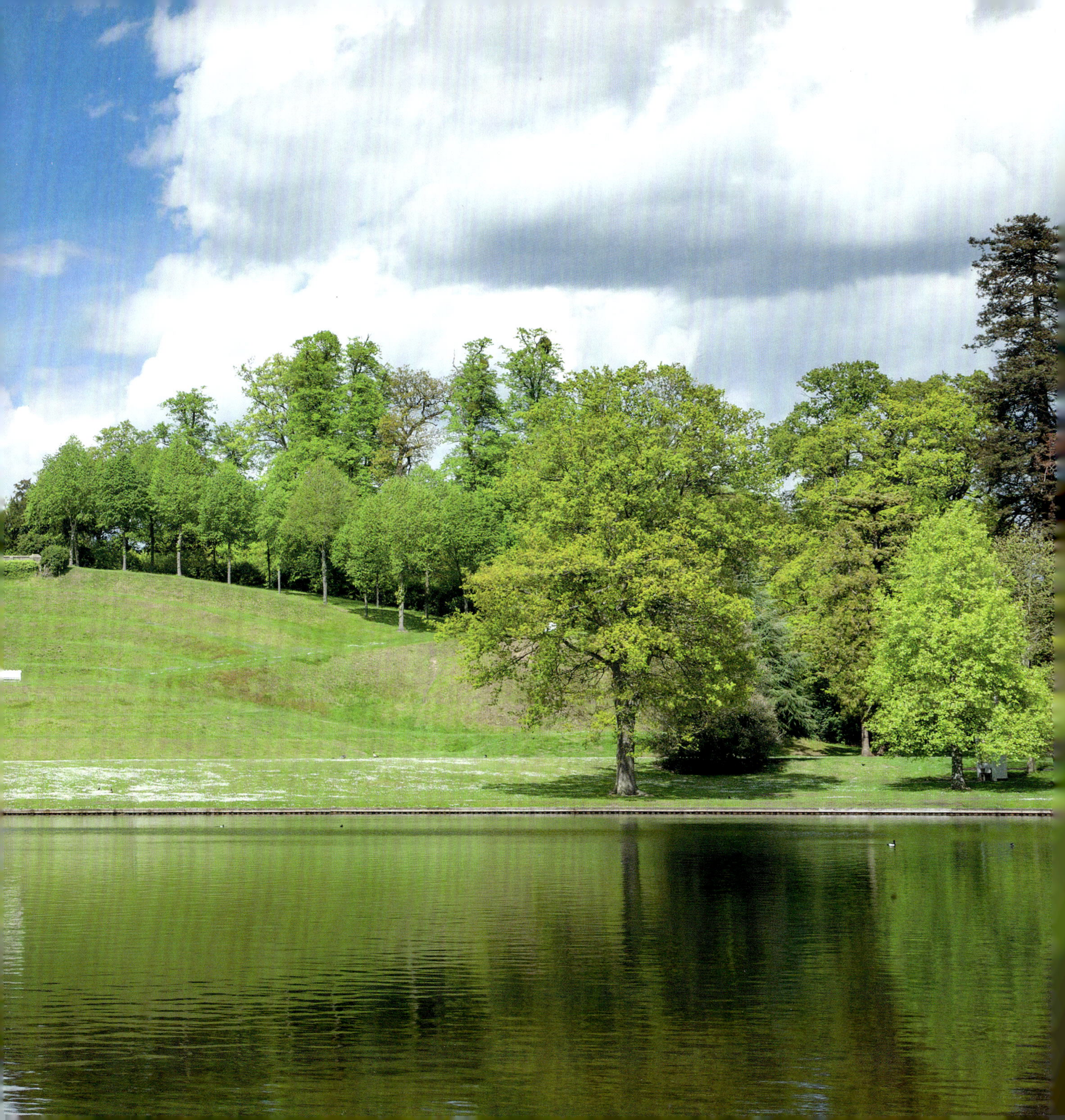

Robert Clive of India

Clive of India was, and still is, a controversial figure in British history. A Major-General in the British East India Company, he fought many campaigns in India and accumulated great wealth in the process.

'A charming new house'

Robert, Lord Clive and his wife Margaret bought Claremont from the Duchess of Newcastle in 1769. The sale price was £25,000 plus the £15,000 that the Newcastles already owed to the Clives. Clive suffered from asthma, and so he pulled down the damp old house and commissioned 'Capability' Brown to design a new one on higher ground. Lady Clive wrote in anticipation, 'You know how pleased I should be to enter a charming new house with a charming old husband'.

At Lord Clive's instruction, or at 'Capability' Brown's suggestion, the route of the Portsmouth Road, which bordered the garden here at its western edge, was changed to increase privacy in the garden. Sadly, Lord Clive died in November 1774 and did not spend a single night under the roof of his new house.

Above The peacock features on the Clive family coat of arms

Far left Design for the entrance front of Claremont House

Left Robert Clive of India; by Nathaniel Dance, c.1770

'The wildest of all her race'

In 1787 Claremont was sold to John, Lord Delaval, the owner of Vanbrugh's great Northumbrian house, Seaton Delaval, which is now also in the care of the National Trust. Delaval gave Claremont to his wayward daughter Sarah and her husband, the 2nd Earl of Tyrconnel, but Sarah was soon openly carrying on affairs with her neighbours, the Duke of York and the Earl of Strathmore. The desolate Strathmore gave his mistress a lavish funeral when she died from TB in 1800 at the age of only 37.

Left Margaret, Lady Clive; by Nathaniel Dance. Music was an important part of her life

Above The wayward Sarah Delaval, Countess of Tyrconnel lived at Claremont from 1787 until her death in 1800; painting attributed to Edward Alcock, 1780s

'A delightful place.'
Robert Clive on Claremont

Royal Claremont

Between 1816 and 1922 Claremont was a much-loved home to British and foreign royalty.

Princess Charlotte and Prince Leopold

Princess Charlotte of Wales and Prince Leopold were married in 1816 and received Claremont, a 'most fit royal residence', as a wedding present from Parliament. The cost was £56,000.

It was at Claremont that the young couple embarked on married life, overcoming any initial 'awkwardness' in each other's company. Princess Charlotte helped 'Leo' with his English (his first language was German), whilst they made ambitious improvements to the gardens at Claremont.

The Camellia House was one of the first greenhouses of its kind: a place to grow and study specimen plants and also somewhere 'the happy couple were to retire after dinner to take their coffee'. It was here that Charlotte spent 'summer evenings under an awning … with his Royal Highness, with a book in her hand'. A pink and white bloomed camellia was named after Princess Charlotte in 1834. The building was demolished in 1959, but some of the original camellias survive on what is now called the Camellia Terrace.

'Claremont … which I am delighted at; it is such a fine thing…'
Princess Charlotte

'A *real paradise*. I was [shown] quite over the house and kitchen garden which is *princely*, and I am quite clear it is the *most fit royal residence* that can be found anywhere.'

Princess Charlotte

Above The Camellia Terrace still contains some of Princess Charlotte's original plants

Right Princess Charlotte and Prince Leopold were married at Carlton House in London on 2 May 1816

Opposite Princess Charlotte and Prince Leopold in the royal box at Covent Garden; engraving by W.T. Fry, 1817

The Bowling Green

Despite living here for only a short time, the young but strong-willed princess made many changes and improvements, including a gravel path round the garden and park for her 'little pony-cart, in which it was her daily practice to ride'.

Given that Princess Charlotte ordered the then unfashionable skittle alley to be removed, we can only assume that bowls were no longer played on the Bowling Green. Growing plants was more to her taste, and so the ground floor of the Belvedere on the hill was made into a conservatory.

'A constant and never-failing source of amusement.'

Princess Charlotte

'My Charlotte is gone'
The tragic death of a future queen

Although George III had fifteen children, Princess Charlotte of Wales was his only legitimate grandchild and second in line to the British throne.

Princess Charlotte died after giving birth to a still-born son here at Claremont on 6 November 1817, aged just 21. If the child had lived, he would have become King of England and there would have been no Victorian age. The national outpouring of grief matched that for a later princess of Wales. Indeed, it was so extreme that linen-drapers across Britain ran out of black cloth for mourning dress. Her devastated husband, Prince Leopold, responded to this tide of emotion by opening Claremont to visitors. Charlotte's cloak was left hanging in the hall of Claremont House just where she had put it when she came in from her last walk in the garden.

On the terrace above the Amphitheatre once stood a tea house that remained unfinished at Princess Charlotte's death. As a tribute to his wife, Prince Leopold had it remodelled as a mausoleum by A. W. N. Pugin and dedicated to her memory. Inside stood a bust of the Princess, and surrounding it, a small flower garden. Princess Charlotte's Mausoleum was demolished in 1922.

Right *The Apotheosis of Princess Charlotte*; by Henry Howard, 1818 (Petworth House). Clutching her dead child, Princess Charlotte is carried heavenwards by angels

Royal Claremont

'Every household throughout Great Britain had lost a favourite child.'

Henry Brougham

The royal rose
A Rose of loveliest form and hue,
In Britain's royal garden grew,
   Its ornament and pride;
Delighted on its charms we gaz'd,
When fate the whelming tempest rais'd –
   It budded, and it died!

Charlotte's death in childbirth in 1817 provoked a wave of national grief.

Commemorative bust of Princess Charlotte, 1819

'England, that great country, has lost everything in losing my ever beloved daughter.'

Queen Caroline

20

Royal Claremont

Young Victoria
An extraordinary woman searching for an ordinary life

Victoria was born a princess and destined to become not only Queen of England, but ruler of the largest empire the world had ever seen.

As a child, Queen Victoria lived a secluded and suffocating life at Kensington Palace, plagued by her overbearing mother. For Victoria, staying with her uncle Leopold at Claremont was a blessed release and a rare opportunity to enjoy some freedom to sketch and play outside.

The garden once resounded with the happy sounds of Princess Victoria 'running and jumping'. One May evening in 1830 visitors to Claremont encountered the princess in the park: 'Out of the dappled shade trotted a child of eleven on a grey pony followed by a white dog. Her hair was long and flowing, her eyes shone and she looked at the strangers with inquisitive surprise.'

When she became a mother, Queen Victoria returned to Claremont with her husband Albert, the Prince Consort, to relive those precious memories, and to give her children a taste of the normality and freedom that she had so longed for.

Opposite Queen Victoria as a child, 1830; by Richard Westall

Above right The young Princess Victoria drew this watercolour sketch of the Claremont gypsies in 1836, a year before she became queen. She sent them blankets and soup, and contrasted their obvious affection for one another with her own unhappy childhood

'The *happiest* days of my otherwise *dull* childhood.'

Queen Victoria on her time at Claremont

A royal family in exile

In 1848 the French king Louis-Philippe was overthrown. He and his family sought refuge in England, deciding to settle at Claremont at Leopold's invitation. Despite the cold and damp, they soon made themselves comfortable. Louis-Philippe died in 1850, but his Queen, Marie-Amélie, lived on at Claremont until her death in 1866.

This corner of Surrey was already attracting property developers, much to the horror of

Above Ex-King Louis-Philippe's sons, the Comte de Paris and Robert d'Orléans riding in the garden at Claremont about 1849; by Alfred Dedreux (château de Versailles)

Right Prince Leopold, 1st Duke of Albany, who lived at Claremont from 1879 until his early death in 1884; with his daughter, Princess Alice, later Countess of Athlone; photograph by Hills & Saunders

Right Portraits of Louis-Philippe, King of the French, and his wife Marie-Amélie appear on these Sèvres vases of 1845

Queen Victoria, who was granted the Claremont estate by Parliament for her lifetime. After making much-needed improvements to both the house and the garden, in 1879 she passed Claremont on to her fourth son, the sickly Prince Leopold (later Duke of Albany). Albany died of a brain haemorrhage in 1884 at the age of only 30. The widowed Duchess remained the tenant of Claremont until her death in 1922, but she lived abroad for much of that period, allowing the house to be used as a military hospital during the First World War.

The breakup of the estate

In 1922 most of the Claremont estate was sold for housing development. All that remained were the house and the surrounding 210 acres of garden and park. Princess Charlotte's Mausoleum and the Temple by the Nine-Pin Alley were demolished, and the house might have gone the same way, if it had not been converted into a school in 1930, now Claremont Fan Court School (not open to visitors).

In 1949 the surviving 49 acres of the garden were given to the National Trust through the National Land Fund.

The National Trust

For the next two decades Claremont was run by Esher Urban District Council. The grass paths were mown and the trees maintained, but there was little money to spend on the fragile garden buildings. During this period the Camellia House and Boat House succumbed to vandalism and had to be demolished. In the late 1960s the National Trust belatedly decided to take the garden back in hand, having realised that the Duke of Newcastle's garden was one of the most significant examples of its kind.

With the help of a grant from the Slater Foundation and the efforts of volunteers the lake was dredged, and Belisle and the Thatched Cottage were repaired. The Amphitheatre was cleared of invasive scrub to reveal its beauty and impressive scale. Research and restoration continue so that visitors can once again take pleasure in this famous pleasure ground.

A fête champêtre at Claremont